First published in

Artwork by Angela Denore.

The PurpleDoor
Bold Street
Liverpool
www.thedoorisopen.co.uk

To anyone who has been searching for something like this and waiting for it to appear.

INTRODUCTION

Do you sometimes feel as if the world's gone mad? From Coronavirus to Brexit, nothing seems to make sense any more, and sometimes things seem to change so fast that it can be difficult to keep up.

Whether or not things are any more crazy now than they were in the past, or whether social media just makes it seem that way, the world is a quick-moving place, where ideas and knowledge can move and change in the blink of an eye. Sometimes change takes decades, sometimes seconds. Social media can make this feel worse - everybody seems to be talking about topics you have never even heard of, and what's more, everyone seems so much more clued up on it than you are.

Relax.

It's ok.

We're here to help.

It can be intimidating to be told to educate yourself if you don't know where to start. Sometimes the views of our parents are out of date, and sometimes the things we were taught in school have changed, or developed. How are we supposed to know that things are different? It can sometimes feel as if you're playing by the wrong set of rules, and on social media, saying the wrong thing can be disastrous.

This is the reason why we created this book. We believe that most people want to understand the way the world works, but sometimes don't know where to start. Especially if we've grown up around very different opinions, it can sometimes be quite a challenge to recognise that we need to do some more research to really understand an issue. We are all different, and this is what makes us unique, but sometimes these differences have been weaponised to turn us against one another through fear, prejudice and scaremongering.

The truth is, if we can understand one another better, we can all get along better. When we take away the inaccuracy and the misinformation, our horizons are opened and we can feel that we belong and that we have a part to play in the world. Sometimes, all it takes is that first step.

This short guide attempts to bring together some of the most pressing issues facing the world today. To keep it pocket sized, we have had to be selective. By no means is this meant to be the final word on these issues, but simply the very first step. In writing about issues as diverse and varied as gender, immigration and disability, we believe it is essential to allow people who most identify with these issues to be the ones to tell you about it. What we want to achieve, in this small guide, is for you to feel comfortable reading about issues which you may not know much about - so that our authors can help you start a journey to break down any gaps in your knowledge. I have created a very difficult task for our contributors by asking them to write only very brief guides to complex topics, and my hope is that this guidebook will direct you towards more learning and more engagement. You will find a full list of recommendations at the end of the book. As with the chapters, these were picked by the authors themselves, and as far as possible, we have tried to provide links to information which you can access for free.

I'm incredibly proud of the diverse range of voices who have been brave enough to tell you something of their own stories in these pages. I hope you enjoy hearing about their different perspectives on life, and I am convinced that even a short read will help you to learn a lot. That was certainly the case for me.

There is nothing more powerful than educating ourselves to learn more about the world in which we live. The more we learn, the more we realise what we have in common. Learning more about each other makes us more empathetic, more welcoming and more of an ally. We live in a world with deep divisions, and by taking the first steps to find out why, I firmly believe we are better prepared to support one another to achieve and to thrive. Thank you for taking these first steps with us.

Karl Falconer

Editor

1.
SELLING NEWS IS A BUSINESS

FAKE NEWS AND THE MEDIA
BY KARL FALCONER

Can you trust the news? It seems as if, ever since Donald Trump became President, we've been hearing about "fake news!" and being told we can't trust the "dishonest" media.

To understand what's really going on, we've got to go back in time. Newspapers have been around in Britain for over 400 years. Imagine: you've started your newspaper empire and business is booming. Your newspapers are flying off the shelves and you're doing important work. Then, one day, across the street, you notice another news agent open. He's a lot younger than you, his newspapers are smaller than yours, and easier to handle. Instead of important news about the King and latest tax reforms, he's got celebrity gossip and naked women in his newspaper. And people are buying it! In fact, he seems to be doing so well that you decide to get in on the act.

Selling news is a business, and business only works if people like you and me buy papers. News is what happened, but selling the news is business. Which newspaper are you going to buy, the one with the factual, boring title, or the one that catches your eye? This has led newspapers to become more and more imaginative with the way they sell their product. In 1903, *The Daily Mirror* started a revolution in newspaper history with the first ***tabloid***. In 1970, *The Sun* printed the first edition of its infamous Page 3 feature. Tabloid newspapers were sensational, focussing on celebrity and gossip - content they claimed readers really wanted to hear about; not politics and finance. The owners of tabloid newspapers became incredibly rich, and a few, most notably Rupert Murdoch, the Australian owner of newspapers including *The Sun* and *The News of the World*, went on to own vast news empires across the world. Because competition was encouraged, media moguls such as Murdoch ended up controlling a ***monopoly***: where one company owns most of the market and competitors are unlikely to break through. At one point, Rupert Murdoch, who was also involved with Fox in America, and Sky here in the UK, was responsible for one quarter of the world's entire news output.

With so much power, comes a problem.

Men like Murdoch became super rich and powerful, as the heads of some of the biggest companies on earth. With this came political leverage. Like many in big business, they favoured governments who kept taxes low, and didn't interfere in their business. As their influence grew, the need to sell more papers increased, and their tactics got less and less honourable. The hounding pressures of the paparazzi are widely blamed for the death of Princess Diana. The impact of *The Sun*'s deliberately misleading headline about Liverpool fans at the Hillsborough disaster rumbles on to this day, with a blanket ban across the Merseyside region. More recently, phone-hacking scandals have emerged, and it has been claimed that the real political force in Britain lies with Rupert Murdoch. *The New York Times* claims that Murdoch, "remade the world." It is argued, with some justification that if Murdoch supports you, you'll win.

The reality is that news has an ***agenda***. Let's say I throw a pen and it hits you. What's the story? You'll say I threw a pen at you. I'll say it just slipped out of my hand. You'll say I threw it at you because of your political views. I'll say I was actually aiming for the guy behind you. Facts and opinions are slippery, and clever people know how to make their opinions sound like facts. By presenting the facts in a particular way, news items can frame a narrative. By creating an exciting story, news has us hooked.

News isn't just in the papers, of course. At 10pm each evening, millions of us tune in to the news - but which channel do you flick to? Everything you see and hear is a decision, made by a big TV boss, to make the news as interesting, scary and addictive as possible. There's a reason stories about war come first and stories about cats up trees come last. Why? Because they need you to keep watching. When you consider that the vast majority of those bosses are able bodied, straight, middle-class, white men, this becomes a problem.

Consider the BBC. It's formal. The men wear ties, you'll very rarely hear a regional accent. The message is: you can trust us. Whatever we tell you, you should listen. Over on ITV, things are a little different, but you might need to dig a bit to notice. Robert Peston might have his top button undone! Often, the presenter (or, ***anchor*** - an anchor gives stability, durr!) will look into the camera and sigh audibly: clearly, they're as fed up of Brexit as the rest of us. The message? We're all on the same side! We're as irritated by this as you are!

The difference between ITV and the BBC is that ITV relies on advertising to make its money. Those adverts pay Piers Morgan's wages. The BBC, on the other hand, is a public service broadcaster - it's funded by the government and we pay for it through a licence fee. Because of this, it has to be ***impartial*** - it's not supposed to be ***biased***, or in favour, of any particular issue. They can't be shown to be favourable to a political party, for example.

Being aware of this means we can be more active in ensuring that our news broadcasters are doing their job properly. Ofcom, the independent body who are supposed to enforce this, recently wrote that, "as national debates become more polarised, it becomes harder for broadcasters to be seen to be accurate and impartial."

To be fair, it's actually harder than you might think to be impartial. Take a subject you think really strongly about and try and talk about it factually, without opinion. It isn't easy, right? This article is biased - I've made my own opinions very clear and I've not given the other side of the argument a chance to have their say. The fact is: we're human, and we're programmed to have opinions - it's a key part of how we fit in. The BBC's mission to be impartial is very difficult in practice, when each of their presenters, directors and management have their own political views and opinions. In short: when they're human too.

Social media has made it easier for ***fake news*** to spread. ***Clickbait*** titles - which will try to catch your attention by saying something like "OMG YOU WILL NOT BELIEVE WHAT KYLIE JENNER HAS DONE NOW!" are really just a development from tabloid headlines. As fewer people buy traditional newspapers, more problematic tactics have been used - including Russian trolls generating deliberately misleading content about Hilary Clinton and targeting this at people who can still be persuaded to vote against her. On social media, we tell Facebook what we like, what we agree with, who we fancy, who we hate. We follow people whose opinions we agree with, meaning that it can be hard to see outside of the bubble we've made for ourselves, because everyone we follow likes what we like. "How could somebody vote for *them*? Everybody I know thinks *this*, so *those* people must be idiots."

We have all been part of the problem, and we must all be part of the solution. Here's ten easy steps we can all take to be more aware of the news we share:

- Think about who's posting. Are they someone you trust?
- Have you read the article you're about to share or just the headline?
- Is there another side of the argument?
- Is it a ***fact*** or an ***opinion***? A fact is something that cannot be proven false: Athens is the capital of Greece, for example.
- Remember that all news has an agenda. The more you click and share, the more money they make. Why are they posting this?
- Check the dates. Is this news current? Just because it was true yesterday doesn't mean it will be today.
- Look out for bias. Consider this sentence: "Apple is obviously the biggest company in the world because everyone has an iPhone." This *might* be true, but I

could equally say that everybody I know owns a Samsung. Is Apple the biggest company in the world? How are we measuring size? The number of employees? The amount of profit? The amount of tax paid?

- Common sense! "5G Spreads Coronavirus," is a typical example of internet hysteria. Not only is it not true, if you know anything about how virus' spread, it makes no scientific sense. All it takes is a quick Google search to check.

- OMG SHARE THIS CONSPIRACY THEORY ABOUT FACEBOOK YOU WILL NOT BELIEVE. This kind of post, usually found on Facebook, is always, absolutely, completely, without a shadow of a doubt, a scam. These posts are designed to confuse you and get you to share them. BUT OMG THIS IS SERIOUS, IF YOU DON'T REPOST THIS WITHIN FIVE MINS THE GOVERNMENT WILL SHUT DOWN YOUR ACCOUNT. There was a recent conspiracy that Boris Johnson's letters were infected with Coronavirus so that we'd all catch it. Take a step back, put your common sense hat on, and think about how ridiculous these sound.

- Check sources. News anchors will often be reporting on a story and use a line such as, "Labour's policy on Brexit does have strengths, but ***many people*** here are saying that they've completely lost the plot and are fighting amongst themselves." Who is saying this? How do we know they didn't just make it up? Could they be making it up so that it'll help push their own agenda?

News and knowledge are tricky things - even the order in which things are presented can impact how we learn about them. It's important to be cautious about all of the information you consume, and to think about whether you can trust it before you share it. When I was at school, we were taught that Pluto was a planet: now science has decided it is not. Knowledge can change as time goes by, which is why educating ourselves, throughout our life, is so important. You only have to go back a few decades to find textbooks, actually used in schools, which were filled with racial stereotypes and hatred: and these were used as part of the science curriculum. Questioning where our information comes from, asking ***who*** wrote it and, importantly, ***why***, is essential.

It's important to remember when our own knowledge is challenged, that the world doesn't really work like a headline, where people are either good or evil. Most of the time, history and life is complicated. We must resist the temptation to refer to things in such simple ways, and accept that people who we admire, like Winston Churchill for instance, can have done really good things for our country, as well as some bad things. It's the same with news. None of us are a headline, we're much more complicated and interesting than that. Take that with you as you read on and enjoy getting to read beyond the clickbait.

2.

WHAT SCHOOL DIDN'T TEACH US

BLACK HISTORY + RACISM

BY PHILIPPA MWAYI

The resurfacing of the ***Black Lives Matter*** moment, sparked by the murder of George Floyd, has resulted in drastic action across the world. From statues being torn down to protests across the globe, people are doing everything they can for their voices to be heard.

Why there is such outrage may not be apparent to everybody, as racism is rarely portrayed as a problem in the UK. If you believed this to be true, you are not alone, and we have our education system to thank for the misinformation.

Despite the UK playing a substantial role in the enslavement of Black people, and despite police brutality and murder still taking place in the UK, and despite the

British colonising African countries, there is virtually no mention of this in our school curriculum. We are often taught about the triumphs of the UK - and there are plenty to celebrate. But to skim over tragedies that Britain has caused leaves many of us naive to the full story.

It's helpful to think of your relationship with the UK in the same way you would a close friend or family member. To ignore the mistakes they make because you love them allows them to continue making them. Calling a loved one out on their mistakes allows them to become a better person and allows your relationship to grow stronger. Similarly, criticising the UK's past does not make you less patriotic, it allows us to move forward and ensure our country is truly one to be proud of.

Let's take a look at some key parts of British history that we have been misinformed about until now.

The Abolishment of Slavery

Black people often hear a range of dismissive responses when they try to discuss the horrific stories of slavery. From being told not to "dwell on the past," to arguing that because Britain was one of the first countries to abolish slavery, we don't need to keep discussing it.

The Slavery Abolition Act instated in 1833 did formally free 800,000 people. However, what is less well known, is that the same act contained a clause stating that each slave owner should be given financial compensation for the loss of their "property". Despite former slaves receiving not a penny of compensation, £20 million (the present-day equivalent of £17 billion) was agreed upon to give to slaveowners as compensation for their loss. The government had to borrow money to pay the 46,000 slave owners. British tax payers were paying off this debt until 2015.

Imagine discovering as a Black British citizen, that the money you have worked so hard to earn, was being used to pay back slave owners. Some of which may have owned, abused and murdered the ancestors of those same taxpayers. We even have statues of many of these slave owners in cities and towns, a frequent reminder of how a sinister past continues to be glorified. With information like this, it should be clear to see why discussing slavery is not dwelling on the past, the effects are still felt now.

"Heroic" Leaders

If there is one thing we are taught a lot about in school, it is Britain's triumph during the war. Many of us have taken that sense of pride and achievement into our adulthood and idolise many war heroes. But what if some of those heroes also had a dark past?

Take Winston Churchill. We know of him as the glorious leader that successfully led us through WW. Whilst this is true, we must also acknowledge that it wasn't all positive. He believed that White people were the superior race and openly stated that he hated Indian people, believing them to be "beastly people with a beastly religion." These opinions fuelled his policies, which had disastrous impacts for world progress, such as the ***Bengal Famine***. In 1943, millions of people were dying of starvation in Bengal, primarily due to large-scale exports of food from India for consumption in the UK. *Churchill's Secret War*, a book by Madhusree Mukerjee, elaborates in further detail, explaining that Churchill and his associates could have easily helped but refused. Churchill suggested that the blame should lie with Indian people for "breeding like rabbits."

You would be right in thinking that extremist views such as these weren't uncommon at the time. However, just because they were common, it does not mean they were innocent: there are countless records, throughout history, of people acknowledging that their actions were inhumane but deciding, ultimately, that profit was more important. It is therefore vital that we don't disregard the consequences of these views. If we think back to the friend analogy, critiquing and raising awareness of Churchill's life and legacy does not mean the positives are no longer recognised. It simply allows us to be better educated about British history. Most would agree that a truly admirable leader would not be responsible for the death of innocent people, nor withhold racist opinions. By knowing the full story behind some of our most famous figures, we can choose even better ones in the future. Ones that want the best for every British citizen, not just those who are White.

Windrush

On 22nd June 1948, the ***MV Empire Windrush*** ship brought hundreds of workers over from Jamaica, Trinidad and Tobago to the UK. In response to post-war labour shortages in Britain, job adverts were created to bring in workers from these countries. Despite what we are often taught about immigration, the UK *needed* these people: not the other way around. Jamaica was, and is, a country not in need of salvation. The UK was desperate for their labour and support to rebuild after the war, but the treatment of the migrants upon arrival was not one of gratitude.

Many passengers paid £28 (close to £1000 today) for transportation to work here. Alongside an estimated 500,000 others who travelled to the UK between 1948 and 1971, in return for their hard work, they were promised better, more prosperous lives. This was not the case. Upon arrival, many suffered from racism and discrimination. Companies refused to hire them because they were Black, landlords refused to provide housing and many were subject to violent abuse and attacks. Despite being promised so much and leaving behind their families to help rebuild Britain, they received anything but a warm welcome.

At the time, they were told by the government that they could stay in the UK permanently. However, the government did not keep a proper record of them. In 2012, when a change in immigration law happened, many members of the Windrush generation did not have the official documents they needed to stay here. This led to many being sent to immigration ***detention centres*** and facing potential ***deportation***.

In 2018, the government issued a formal apology with the reassurance that nobody would be forced to leave. But by this point, the damage had been done. Despite dedicating so many years of their lives to contributing to this country, this treatment highlighted how little they were valued. With this happening so recently, it becomes apparent that racism and discrimination is unfortunately not a thing of the past.

Despite being hard to come to terms with, these few moments are just the tip of the iceberg. There is a whole side of British history – our shared history – that has been hidden from us for so long. When you learn that in 2018, 85.9% of all teachers in state-funded schools in England are White British, it is no surprise that our knowledge of the country we live in is one-sided. Whilst there is the potential for the curriculum to function properly and teach us the full story, in the meantime, our only option is to teach ourselves and relearn the past.

To ignore the past does not make it go away and Black people do not have the luxury of ignoring years of oppression and discrimination that are directly responsible for the inequalities we see in society today. We all know the past cannot be changed but by being aware of it and not just the good parts, we can learn from it. We can stop the same things happening again, we can ensure the voices and struggles of Black people are finally recognised. Most importantly, we can do better.

3.

BEING HONEST OR BEING SAFE

SEXUALITY

BY JEN CAMPION

L*GBTQIA+* represents, not a delicious and very large sandwich (although I'd love to try that), but the spectrum of human sexuality. This is such a huge topic that it's not surprising it gets bogged down in acronyms. The important thing to remember is that we love who we love and we can't help it; it's written in our genes.

As a teenager in rural Devon during the early 00s, I thought everyone felt the same way I did about Avril Lavigne, and that the butterflies I felt upon walking into GCSE Chemistry reflected my burning passion for the subject (spoiler alert: it was more to do with Miss Smith, who had long black hair and an American accent). It was staring me in the face and I couldn't get my head around it. I didn't know anyone who was gay and there was very little LGBT representation in popular culture. At this time it was common to describe anything uncool as being "gay" e.g "those shoes are so gay." It may seem small, but this kind of language reinforces the idea that gay = bad. It's the bottom rung of a ladder that builds up to painful and dangerous discrimination.

What Does LGBT Stand For?

L - ***Lesbian***. A woman who is attracted to other women.

G - ***Gay***. Usually applied to men, it can also describe women who are attracted to the same sex.

B - ***Bisexual***. Someone who is attracted to men and women.

T - ***Transgender*** - this is covered in Chapter 6!

Q - ***Queer*** - Queer was a pejorative term until LGBT groups in the 1990s reclaimed it. This form of empowerment removes the negative associations with the word. It has since become more common for members of the LGBT community to identify as queer. Q can also stand for ***Questioning***, representing those who are exploring their sexuality.

I - ***Intersex***. This term describes people who are born with anatomy that doesn't clearly fit the definition of male or female.

A - ***Asexual*** (sometimes called Ace). Someone who doesn't prioritise sex in a relationship. They may not enjoy sex with anyone, or they might as part of a committed relationship. An ace person can still have romantic feelings, fall in love, and enjoy other physical affection such as holding hands.

+ - The plus sign, which represents identities, for example ***pansexual*** (attraction regardless of sex/ gender). Using the plus sign is a good way to ensure you include everyone.

Why All The Labels?

It might seem like new labels are being added all the time. And some people aren't fans - including members of the LGBT community. However, for many people it is helpful to have a word to describe themselves and this forms an important part of personal identity. At the end of the day, it doesn't hurt anyone, but it helps lots of people.

But What Do I Call You?

Saying "the LGBT community" is a pretty good catch-all term, although I know it doesn't exactly roll off the tongue. In terms of individuals, it's best to follow their lead. So long as you're respectful and listen, you can't go wrong.

Sexuality is Not a Choice or a Disease

It is not possible to socialise a person into being LGBT, because sexuality is not a choice. We know this because the numbers of LGBT identifying people are pretty consistent across tolerant and less tolerant societies. If it was a social thing, you would expect higher numbers in more tolerant countries. After all, why would so many people choose to have fewer rights?

Being LGBT is not a sickness that can be cured, which is why so-called "***conversion therapy***" does not work and has been denounced by the NHS and the British Association for Counselling and Psychotherapy, among others. Maybe it seems like there are more of us around these days, but that's because we're not hiding.

Coming Out

Although we have made a lot of progress, ***heterosexuality*** is still seen as the norm and so ***coming out*** is a process that the majority of LGBT people have to go through. Coming out to your loved ones is scary and emotional. It can be positive and life affirming, however unfortunately not everyone is accepted by their families and some young people are even forced to leave home.

Coming out doesn't happen just once: it happens over and over again, every time you meet someone new. The taxi driver, making small talk, who asks where your husband works, or the hotel receptionist booking you into a double room. Sometimes you have to choose between being honest or being safe.

Even today, it's not always safe to be out. A 2017 Stonewall survey found that 1 in 5 people had experienced a hate crime incident within the last 12 months. Hard-won gains, such as the legalisation of ***same-sex marriage***, are the result of decades of fighting.

Sexuality is a Spectrum

No identity is a finite box that we have to stay in forever. Sexuality can change throughout life, and everyone is somewhere on the spectrum. Imagine a line with "Gay" at one end and "Heterosexual" on the other: most of us fall somewhere in between those points.

Being straight is normalised only within a society which chooses to normalise it, and LGBT people have been present in all cultures, forever (Ancient Rome, anyone?). The terminology might change, but the inherent truth of our existence does not.

4.

WE ALL HAVE MENTAL HEALTH

MENTAL HEALTH
BY JESSICA CLARK

We don't need no education... Or perhaps we do...

When I was at school, there was no education about mental health. The 30-minute weekly PSHE sessions in our otherwise academic timetable grazed over discussions of bullying and harrowing videos of teenagers who had died from ecstasy overdoses (as well as scarring lists of STDs and the legendary condom-banana demonstration). Between 1993 - 2018, the number of deaths related to ecstasy use in England and Wales averaged 40 per year. Yet in 2018 alone, ***suicide*** (depression's most drastic and tragic manifestation) accounted for 6,507 deaths in the UK. If we are to be warned about the harmfulness of recreational drug-taking, why are we taught nothing about managing the far more prevalent and insidious threat of mental illness, given its statistical likelihood to be experienced by 25% of the classroom across our lifetimes? *All* of us have mental health, which exists on a spectrum and can change with time. Sometimes our mental health is good, other times it needs some support, and if we talk about mental health when it's good, it's easier to talk about when its bad. Being aware of this is important, given the ease with which some people label mental health, and its challenges, as something that "happens to other people."

My Experience

I did not consider the urgent need for more clarity, openness, and readily available information on mental health until my early twenties, when I sank into a depressive episode during my university year abroad. I had known brief bouts of melancholic states and debilitating ***anxiety*** previously but never to such an extreme level. I believe that better education about the symptoms and triggers of ***depression*** and how to access support during a crisis could have significantly aided my years-long journey involving an array of antidepressant medications, psychiatry, shamanic healing, and plenty of tears and sleepless nights. It has helped me colossally to understand clinical depression as a human experience undergone by many others, not just myself.

Of the many different approaches for treating depression and anxiety, no single school of thought contains a fix-all toolkit. Rather, different positive coping mechanisms and nuggets of wisdom can be gleaned from the range of treatments and literature available to evolve one's own methods of recovery, a process to be handled with as much patience and self-love as possible. Creating space to talk with those around you about what you are going through, as well as contacting your GP, are commendable first steps. Realising you're in need of support can be the hardest first step, but the key to unlocking the rest of your recovery. Physical health, a balanced lifestyle, and support from loved ones all go a long way in aiding the recovery path.

Mental Health Today

- Mental health accounts for over half of all sickness-related work absences in the UK.
- One in four people in the UK will suffer from a mental health problem at some point in their lives.
- According to a GOV UK survey, 7.3 million people (nearly 20% of the adult population) were prescribed ***antidepressants*** in the year 2017/18.
- The Coronavirus pandemic has seen a dramatic increase in the number of people seeking support.
- Suicide is the biggest killer of men under 50. 84 men a week die by suicide, which is the equivalent of 1 every 2 hours.
- Suicide is the biggest killer of pregnant women and mothers with children under 1.

Stigma and Misconceptions

Stigma is a sense of shame, social disgrace and personal culpability associated with mental health problems. It is something ingrained within our cultural beliefs and societal norms, and many sufferers continue to face stigma in spite of campaigns to promote better awareness. Stigma does not affect all equally: for example, men face more stigma than women when talking openly about mental health, due to stereotypical notions of masculinity. Prolific writers, activists and organisations continue to bring mental health conversation into the mainstream to eradicate stigma and ensure that nobody has to suffer in silence. A sense of stigma can prevent people from accessing, what would otherwise be a positive recovery process.

Some misconceptions about depression and anxiety, the most common mental illnesses in the UK, include:

- That they have to be "about" a specific occurrence in one's life. Depression and anxiety can affect anyone at any point in their lives.
- That they are equivalent to regular emotional experiences of sadness and worry.
- That they are not that serious. What have you got to be sad about?
- That they are experienced in the same way by all sufferers.

- That wealth, status, career or personal relationships can make one immune. One of the great paradoxes of depression and anxiety is that they can spring up even when somebody has lots of objectively positive or desirable things in their life.
- That people going through them always understand why they feel the way they do.
- That these health problems are purely experienced psychologically.

Mental Health - A Body Map

But I thought it was all in your head...

Many mental health conditions involve physical symptoms which may register unnoticed to the outside eye. For example....

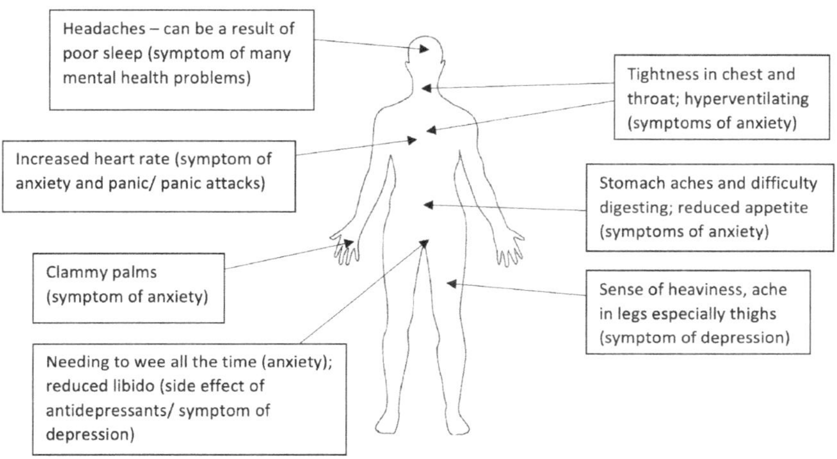

How Can I Support a Loved One in Need?

The pillars of good mental health - a healthy diet, sufficient rest, exercise and meaningful activities in one's day - can be difficult to maintain during a depressive episode. Checking in that your loved one is staying well-nourished and connected to other people (even if in small ways) will be of help to them, though they may find it hard to do these things.

Just hearing a friendly voice on the phone, or in person, can help others to feel less alone. It is worth checking in with your network regularly, as it may not be obvious who is struggling at any given moment. If you can find something to laugh about, all the better! It may be useful to talk through specific areas of their life that could be aggravating their condition, such as a stressful job or relationship problems, and brainstorm practical ways of alleviating excessive pressure. Remember, asking people how they are, and normalising talking about mental health when it is good, makes it easier to talk about when it is bad, especially for those people who may let stigma prevent them from seeking the support they need. Be prepared to listen, and try not to fix someone's problems, or take their mental health issue personally; it may be more valuable to lend your ear as a good listener, while signposting further help. Sufferers of poor mental health are regularly encouraged to talk: but if someone asked you for help would you know what to do? ***The Hub of Hope*** is an excellent resource - you can download it as an app - which pinpoints you towards local providers and emergency support based on your current location.

Getting together to engage in a low-energy activity, like watching a film or having a walk, can be beneficial. Films, books, plays and music can all generate positive sources of distraction from mental distress.

5.

KNOW YOUR RIGHTS

HUMAN RIGHTS

BY MOLLY-MAY SMITH

What are human rights?

Human rights are founded on the idea that everyone should be able to live a fair, free and dignified life. They ensure human beings have a degree of protection from unfair and inhumane treatment.

Human rights apply equally to all human beings, no matter who you are or where you're from. Neither your government nor another person can take them away from you, but sometimes they can be restricted or violated.

Human rights aren't just theoretical - they're often protected by law. Today, we understand human rights through the Universal Declaration of Human Rights.

What is the Universal Declaration of Human Rights?

Following the atrocities committed during World War II, the ***Universal Declaration of Human Rights*** (UDHR) was drawn up in 1948 to attempt to unify all the countries in the world. All 192 members of the ***United Nations*** signed the Universal Declaration of Human Rights.

Here are a few examples of human rights, all of which are set out by the Universal Declaration of Human Rights. They cover economic, social, cultural, civil and political rights.

- You should never be discriminated against for any reason. Rights belong to all people, whatever our differences.
- No-one shall be subjected to torture or to cruel, inhumane or degrading treatment or punishment.
- You have the right to be treated by the law in the same way as everyone else.
- You have the right to marry and to raise a family.
- You have the right to practice your religion freely.
- You have the right to freedom of opinion and expression.
- You have the right to take part in and choose the government of your country.

- You have the right to work, to good working conditions, to get a fair salary, to equal pay for equal work and to form and join unions.
- You have the right to a decent life, including enough food, clothing, housing, medical care and social security.
- You have the right to an education.

What's the Problem?

Despite all countries in the United Nations signing the Universal Declaration of Human Rights, it's not legally binding and some don't observe their responsibility and continue to violate people's freedoms and dignity. Most governments have made efforts to integrate human rights and ideas of equality and fairness into their legal systems to ensure they're enforced.

How are Human Rights Enforced?

It falls to the individual state to secure human rights in their own countries and take the necessary measures to ensure they are respected. Most states have incorporated elements of the Universal Declaration of Human Rights into their constitutions or legal systems. But even amongst the governments that have, there are still examples of human rights violations.

UK Human Rights Act

The Human Rights Act gives people a set of laws they can use to support their case in a UK court. It was passed by Parliament in 1998.

Sometimes we associate human rights abuses with different countries, but this is a myth. This idea can be quite damaging and leads people to think that the UK is innocent, or that human rights abuses only happen in other parts of the world - but human rights violations happen everyday in the UK.

European Convention on Human Rights

An international treaty signed by 47 European states, who all made a legal commitment in 1950. Member countries and citizens from across the EU can bring cases to the ***European Court of Human Rights***. Any decisions made by the court are usually respected and enforced by member states.

UN Human Rights Council

The UN Human Rights Council can investigate human rights violations and make recommendations, but they can't force countries to change a policy or seek justice for victims.

Know Your Rights

It seems simple, but it's powerful. Knowing the rights and freedoms you and others are entitled to arms you with the knowledge to challenge injustices and protect yourself and others. Use the ***British Institute for Human Rights'*** tool to learn more about your rights in the UK.

Get Specific

Learn about individual human rights cases in the UK and in the rest of the world. There's a whole host of different types of human rights issues, from ***women's rights*** to the ***death penalty***, you might find something that inspires you to take action.

Hold People in Power Accountable

Organisations will often ask you to support their campaigns in a number of ways on their websites or social media platforms. This could be:

- Signing a petition.
- Sharing information with friends and family and having conversations.
- Joining a protest or public meeting.
- Writing to a Member of Parliament or decision maker.
- Reading further resources to be better informed about human rights issues at home and abroad.

6.

GENDER + SEX ARE A SPECTRUM

TRANS IDENTITIES

BY AL TYRRELL

What does "trans" mean?

Trans is the short form of ***transgender***, an umbrella term to describe anyone whose gender identity is different from the one they were assigned at birth. Basically, ***gender*** - your inner ***identity*** in relation to the characteristics of masculinity and femininity - isn't ***binary***, it can't be divided into two categories. There's not just male and female, but more of a spectrum of genders, with some people feeling like men, some people feeling like women, and some people feeling like neither (and therefore feeling, literally, ***non-binary***). Sex, on the other hand, refers to physical anatomy and is divided into ***male*** and ***female*** on the basis of reproductive function. Everyone in the UK gets "assigned" a gender at birth according to their sex - i.e. labelled "boy" if they have a penis, or "girl" if they have a vagina - and for the majority of people, this works, because their biological sex and inner gender identity lines up. These people are ***cisgender***, or ***cis***. Some people, however, grow up to realise that the gender they've been assigned doesn't match their inner gender identity. These people are ***transgender***.

(Biological sex isn't actually binary either, because not everyone is born with either female or male sex attributes - intersex people are born with genitalia/hormones/ chromosomes that don't fit into either sex category. Both gender and sex exist along a spectrum.)

Trans people may ***transition*** - change themselves outwardly to affirm their inner gender identity - in various ways, from changing names and ***pronouns*** (*she/her, he/him, they/them*), to adopting new hair and clothing, to altering gendered behaviour. Many trans people, but not all, may choose to ***medically transition*** where possible as well. There's no single surgery which constitutes a "sex change" - instead, there are a range of different medical transition options, from ***hormone therapy*** (which causes bodily changes such as breast development or the deepening of the voice), to feminizing or masculinizing **gender-affirming surgeries** for different parts of the body. You should always refer to a trans person by their chosen name and pronouns as soon as they ask you to, regardless of whether their transition is visible to you.

Derogatory Words

The word ***transsexual*** is sometimes used to mean transgender, but it's a bit outdated and medicalised (usually suggesting someone who has medically transitioned). Some trans people might use this word about themselves, but others experience it as derogatory. The word ***transvestite*** refers to a cross-dresser (someone who wears clothing associated with a different gender from their own) and shouldn't be confused with *transgender*; to refer to a trans person as a transvestite is offensive because it reduces their gender identity to a costume. Similarly, ***tranny*** (derived from transvestite), is a derogatory slur, and should never be used by non-trans people.

Common Myths

"Being trans is a new fad - there were no trans people in my day / at my school / where I work."

Not true. Trans people have existed as long as the categories of "man" and "woman" have existed, it's just that trans visibility has increased in the media in recent years. Chances are that there probably were trans people at your school / workplace, just not people who were out. As our understanding of gender has developed and the world has grown (slightly) more accepting of trans people, it's become easier to come out as trans without facing extreme hostility - which is why it seems like many more people are living as trans now than in past decades and centuries. If you're interested, there's a lot of information online about cool trans people who were out and visible going back through the ages!

"Okay, so maybe there are transgender men and transgender women. But *more* than two genders? That doesn't make sense."

Non-binary people (people who do not identify as either men or women) have, just like trans people, been around forever. The word "non-binary" may be new, but the idea itself - that some genders sit outside of the categories of "man" and "woman" - is pretty ancient, with evidence of gender nonconforming people existing across the globe throughout human civilisation. In fact, shamefully, the Western gender binary is something that was forcefully imposed on much of the rest of the world through ***colonialism***, displacing many cultures' richer understandings of gender and its fluidity. If you think about it, the thing that really doesn't make sense is trying to fit everyone in humanity into these two rigid and unimaginative boxes in the first place.

"I want to support trans people, but there are so many new words and names for things that I don't even know where to begin."

The constantly evolving terminology surrounding trans identities can make it feel like an uphill battle trying to stay informed, but the most important thing, more so than learning all the words and terms, is to approach people's identities with an open mind and to respect the words that people ask you to respect. Ask people what name and pronouns they prefer (don't assume), use their chosen name and pronouns even when they aren't around, and correct yourself when you get it wrong. It's totally forgivable not to know all the right words for things off the bat - as long as you're prepared to be open, admit mistakes, and keep educating yourself.

"I support trans rights, but there should be rules about bathrooms to make sure that cisgender men can't get in by *pretending* to be trans."

Violent men don't have to pretend to be trans to assault women - if they want to assault women, they'll do it anyway. And, for that matter, violent men are as much of a risk to men and children in the gents as they would be to women in the ladies. The concept of the cisgender man pretending to be trans is a false threat constructed by Trans Exclusionary Radical Feminists (or TERFs) to try and encourage ***transphobic*** views. In reality, the number of cases of cis men dressing up as women to get into ladies bathrooms is very, very low, whereas the number of cases of ordinary trans people just wanting to use the bathroom they feel comfortable in is very, very high.

"I don't think children should be allowed to alter their bodies at a young age, before they truly know who they are and what they want."

The idea that trans kids can get life-changing surgery is false - trans people can't get gender-affirming surgery before the age of 18 in the UK. For a trans teenager, the process of medical transition begins with several months of appointments with a multidisciplinary ***Gender Identity Development*** team (including a clinical psychologist, child psychotherapist, child and adolescent psychiatrist, family therapist, and social worker). After this, the teen may be approved to take hormone blockers, which pause the physical effects of puberty (like breast development and facial hair growth), and which are reversible. Only after being on hormone blockers for a year can a young trans person begin to take gender-affirming hormones which cause bodily changes that are harder to reverse. The waiting lists for NHS gender services are currently extremely long, with many people waiting years for a first appointment - so there's no chance that a trans kid could possibly rush through the process.

"They/them pronouns? That doesn't work grammatically. It's hard to learn and I'd rather just refer to people with the pronouns I'm used to."

Actually, while it might seem odd to refer to someone with the singular "they" pronoun, it is grammatically correct and it's been in common use since the 1400s. You probably use it all the time without realising, any time you refer to someone without specifying their gender. For example: "My friend's running late but they'll be here soon."; "Look, they've got the same car as you."; "I'll ask the person at the desk if they can change my tickets, unless you want to ask them.'" It can feel pretty weird at first to start referring to someone you think of as "she" or "he" as "they", but once you get used to it, it feels fine. And if someone asks you to use those pronouns, it means it's really important to them. Try, get it wrong a few times, correct yourself, keep trying, and soon you won't be thinking twice about it.

A Few More Words to Know

- ***Non-binary*** - a term to describe someone who doesn't identify as a man or a woman. Non-binary people might see themselves as being both male and female, neither male nor female, or somewhere between male and female. While many non-binary people identify as transgender, not all do. Non-binary people often (but not always) adopt gender-neutral pronouns, most commonly ***they/them.***

- ***Intersex*** - a term to describe someone born with biological attributes that don't fit into either the male or female sex category. Intersex people are often forcibly assigned a sex at birth through surgery, but this practice has become more and more controversial as intersex adults have spoken out against it. In the past, intersex people might have been known as ***hermaphrodites***, but this term is now outdated and derogatory.

- ***Gender dysphoria*** - the feeling of discomfort and distress caused by the mismatch between someone's gender identity and the gender they were assigned at birth. (Not to be confused with ***body dysmorphia***, an anxiety disorder that causes a person to have a distorted view of how they look.) Gender dysphoria is not a mental illness or distortion of perception, but a true and justified feeling that your body does not match up to your inner identity.

- ***TERF*** - Trans Exclusionary Radical Feminist - a transphobic feminist, who might be connected to the radical feminist movement. TERF beliefs tend to manifest around ***gender essentialism***: the scientifically incorrect idea that biological sex is binary and fixed and determines gender, which suggests that trans people don't exist. In particular, TERFs argue that trans women aren't real women and shouldn't be allowed in "women-only" spaces - but this argument is completely flawed, and is primarily used, along with the phrase "women-only space," to exclude and demonise trans women.

- ***Dead name*** - the birthname of a trans person which they no longer use. To ***deadname*** someone is to use this former name rather than the person's chosen name, something which often causes the person discomfort and pain (and may put them in a precarious position if it outs them to others who didn't know that they were trans).

- ***Misgender*** - some pronouns in English are gendered, indicating the gender of the person they refer to: ***he/him*** indicates male, ***she/her*** indicates female, and recently, ***they/them*** has been used to indicate non-binary genders. Trans people often change their pronouns to fit their gender identity (e.g. a trans man who used to be "she" is now "he"). To ***misgender*** someone is to use the wrong pronouns for them, or refer to them as the wrong gender - something which, like deadnaming, can cause the person discomfort and pain. If you make a mistake with pronouns or names, it's best not to make a huge deal out of it and just correct yourself, apologise and move on, so that the person doesn't have to linger on it. It helps after getting it wrong to try and use the right name/pronoun three times in a row, to lodge it in your head, e.g. "*Jay* has a great smile; *Jay* was my first mate at work; I love hanging out with *Jay*", or "It was lovely of Robin to invite me to *their* house tonight; I'll invite *them* to mine next week; we could watch that show *they* suggested."

- ***Trans**** - a written form of "trans" with an asterisk to signal the inclusion of gender nonconforming and non-binary people under the transgender umbrella.

7.
YOU MAKE THE DIFFERENCE

POLITICS AND VOTING
BY NATASHA PRINCE

Politics is all around us and has a daily impact on our lives. This chapter will explore some common questions and views about politics, show you how you can make a difference, and provide some useful resources to further understanding and involving yourself in the political world around you.

What Does Politics Have to do with Me?

It's easy to forget how frequently we come into contact with politics and political decisions. Some of the ways politics may affect your day-to-day life include:

- The price of VAT on your shopping.
- Potholes on your street.

- How much you earn.
- New builds in your community.
- Whether you pay for medical prescriptions.

Why Should I Care?

Because you can make a difference. There are currently twenty-nine Members of Parliament who won their seat by less than one thousand votes, showing just how important participation is. When politics is discussed in the media we are often referred to collectively as "the public," but in reality it is the action of individuals that has a real impact.

At every election each individual gets to choose who they want to represent them. You can quickly find out who your MP is and see how they've been voting on important issues at www.theyworkforyou.com. The laws our MP's vote for or against, impact each of our lives, so knowing whether they supported certain ***bills*** is an empowering way to make sure they're representing you. Most politicians stay with the same ***political party*** their whole life, but as a voter you can change your allegiance as much as you like, depending on whose ***policies*** most align with your beliefs. It can therefore be useful to keep an eye on your MP's voting history, so you can decide if they deserve your vote at the next election.

What is the Difference Between the Main Parties?

Political parties are frequently referred to as being on a "spectrum" which ranges from ***left*** to ***right***, with mainstream UK politics usually landing somewhere near the ***centre***. Different ends of the spectrum relate to different social and economic beliefs, allowing us to easily compare parties. The four biggest parties currently in parliament are:

The Conservative Party

The "***Tories***" are the largest centre-right party in the UK. Notable Conservative leaders include Winston Churchill, Margaret Thatcher, David Cameron, and currently, Boris Johnson. Although over time their ideology has evolved, the Conservatives' policies usually include:

- Limited government interference and increased ***private ownership*** of industries.
- A ***free market*** (this means that the price of services and goods are determined by consumers, and "free" from government intervention).
- Traditional social values, such as family-life.
- Maintenance of England, Scotland, Wales and Northern Ireland as the United Kingdom.

The Labour Party:

Labour are to the centre-left of the political spectrum, and so their policies often (but not always) contrast to the Conservatives. Some famous Labour leaders include

Clement Atlee, Tony Blair, Jeremy Corbyn, and the current leader Sir Kier Starmer. Labour's beliefs have also undergone changes over time, but they are most commonly known for supporting:

- State ownership of industries such as healthcare, transport and broadband - this is known as nationalisation.
- Workers' rights, trade unions and an increased minimum wage.
- High levels of economic state support for social care, including children and the elderly.
- Power given to regional branches of government.

The Liberal Democrats

The Lib Dems reached their height of power in modern history after the 2010 election when they formed a ***coalition*** government with the Conservatives, with their then leader Nick Clegg serving as Deputy Prime Minister. Liberal Democrat policies include equal opportunities for all, and electoral reform, which would change the voting system used in the UK.

The Scottish National Party

The Scottish National Party began to climb the political ladder in 2015. Although they only stand for seats in Scotland, they are (at the time of writing) the third largest party in parliament. It is therefore unlikely for the SNP to form a government alone, however like the Lib Dems, the SNP can be essential to giving the Conservatives or Labour a majority when voting on laws.

These are currently the four largest parties in parliament; smaller parties include the Democratic Unionist Party, Sinn Féin and the Social Democratic and Labour Party in Northern Ireland, Plaid Cymru in Wales, and the Green Party in both Wales and England. When it comes to election time, you can find out what policies each party is proposing by checking out their ***political broadcasts*** on the TV, or by reading their ***manifesto***.

So, we've established the importance of voting, and who you might be voting for, but elections only happen every few years, and political activism outside of elections is just as important. At any time you can:

- Sign a petition. Petitions which reach more than 100,000 signatures have to be debated in Parliament.
- Write to your MP.
- Attend your MP's local surgery.
- Vote in local elections.
- Attend local council meetings.
- Join a political party.

These are just some of the ways to get involved. If you care about an issue, it is almost guaranteed that other people do too, and that they are looking to make real change in communities across the country.

8.

HOW I PERCEIVED MYSELF

DISABILITY

BY ROBYN OLIVIA

When you see the word disability, what do you think of? What image appears in your head?

I will take a guess. I may be completely wrong, but normally it is someone you would see as helpless.

If that is what comes to your mind - that's ok - however, please keep reading because I'd like to share with you some information about the ***Social Model of disability*** - a model that truly changed the way I perceived myself as a disabled woman and other people with disabilities. I hope it may do the same for you.

Let's start with the definitions.

Disability is defined in the dictionary as, "a physical or mental condition that limits a person's movements, senses, or activities." When we talk about disability, we normally talk about it from a medical perspective - meaning that we talk about how the condition affects the individual and what is wrong and how that limits them. The word disability is problematic in itself and has negative connotations. The word suggests that anyone with a disability is lacking in ability. Combine this with the language used to describe those with disabilities ("helpless," "heroic," "wheel-chair bound," "living with...") we find that, maybe without meaning to, this language and the medical view of disability is aiding the stereotypes. Instead of acknowledging that they are, "a person with a disability," our language and the medical view confines them to the sole experience of being a disabled person suggesting, ultimately, the fault for their limited access lies with them.

To give you an example, when I was 18, I went for an open day. On seeing that there was a ballet element to the course I was interested in, I thought - oh shit - when I point my toes on my right foot, it doesn't exactly do that... I looked at my mum, I knew she was thinking the same. However, as optimists, we approached a member of staff. I explained that I have mild right sided ***cerebral palsy*** and certain elements of ballet could be a problem. I asked what support there could be for someone with a disability. In short, she said that if I couldn't do ballet due to my condition, maybe this course wasn't for me.

Now, the medical view of disability agrees with this view. As a woman with cerebral palsy, I would not be able to access this course due to my condition being the problem. Therefore, a career in this area was probably not possible.

If you speak to any person with a disability, you will hear very similar stories.

"Sorry but due to your disability, you can't go to a mainstream school."

"Due to your disability, you will never be able to ride a bike."

"Due to you being in a wheelchair, you can't get on this public transport."

I could go on, but hopefully you see the pattern forming. The blame is placed on the individuals' medical condition.

The social model of disability, however, suggests that the term disability defines disabled people in a way that is broad, vague and often inaccurate to the ability and potential of those labelled. It reinforces that it is not an issue of dis- ability but instead, that society is ***disabling*** those same people due to the ***inaccessibility*** of the culture in which disability has evolved.

As we have already mentioned, language and social attitudes form clear cut definitions. It leads to stereotyping those with disabilities and it is this language and these attitudes that disables them from accessing society. And what about environment? What if I told you that 55% of all London's train stations do not have step free access and that nationwide 40% of stations in England are also inaccessible to those with a ***physical disability***. Can you see that in these situations, a wheelchair user is dis-abled from accessing these train stations? A lack of accessible buildings, services, ***captioning*** and ***interpreters*** create barriers for the individual to participate in mainstream society. They are being dis-abled by the inaccessibility of the world around them.

Einstein once said, "everybody is a genius. But if you judge a fish by its ability to climb a tree, it will live its whole life believing that it is stupid." Disabled people are so often judged and held to the standards of a society that is completely inaccessible for them. It is important for us to learn, together, what the social model of disability is. This model doesn't "blame" the individual or turn them into the problem. It is an ***equal opportunities*** model that allows everyone to collaboratively identify and solve problems surrounding ***accessibility***. It brings disabled people into the conversation. Most importantly, it acknowledges the rights of those with disabilities to have full participation in their society. This model allowed me to see and recognise that my disability was not the problem.

How you can help? How can you be an ally to those with disabilities? It all starts with education and language.

- Try not to use words like heroic or brave or to sensationalise our daily experiences - we are not an inspiration just because we woke up and got dressed. Sharing videos like "girl asks disabled boy to prom - isn't she great," can be really hurtful and damaging too.

- Don't be afraid of the word disabled or disabled people. I remember sitting in my wheelchair when I was younger and I was either ignored, stared at like an extra head might pop out on my shoulders, or people would ask my mum, pushing my wheelchair "how is she?" – believing that because I was sat in a wheelchair, I was unable to talk. Talk to us and listen to us.

- Don't assume you know what disability looks like. There is a wide range of disabilities that exist: not all are visible, and each individual has their own experience of their disability, so respect that and listen to what we have to say.

- Advocate for disability rights, lift our voices and help make change in your communities to improve access and representation. Together, through education, we can raise awareness and start changing the way society views those with disabilities.

9.

YOU DON'T LOOK AUTISTIC

AUTISM AND NEURODIVERSITY

BY BETH WESTBROOK

I am autistic. Autism is a ***developmental disability*** which can impact social skills, and how you process the world. I was diagnosed when I was 3 years old, so I have been aware that I am autistic for most of my life. For the first 2 years of education, I was in a ***Special Educational Needs Unit***, and then moved to mainstream education. Being autistic means I am more prone to mental illnesses, and I struggle with anxiety and depression. I struggle if there are a lot of smells around me, and I can't always process sounds.

When you say, "You don't look autistic," I know you mean it as a compliment, but it actually means you may not recognise or understand my struggles, and can't actually support me. It also implies that being "normal" is more desirable and acceptable than being autistic. If I had a pound for every time someone told me, "You don't look autistic," I wouldn't be a millionaire but I could probably have a lovely weekend in Wales.

Despite a popular misconception, vaccinations don't cause autism. If you are considering not vaccinating your child because of the "risk," I'm not here to force my opinions on you, but would you rather a potentially seriously ill child, or an autistic child?

I'm not saying I'd choose to be autistic, but I don't want to cure myself. Some people call autism a superpower, and if that was the case, I guess my superpower would be being having surprise panic attacks, being terrible at maths, and having a blue badge for a car I can't drive. I accept the fact that I am autistic and adapt my world to make life easier. Autism isn't a worst-case scenario. It's a part of my identity I wouldn't change (and can't, it's a lifelong disability, so no injecting bleach into my veins, unfortunately).

Because I am autistic, I am part of the ***neurodiverse community***. Neurodiversity is a long word, but its definition is actually simple. Neurodiversity refers to a community where brains have different behavioural traits and are wired to think and see the world differently. Those people who could be seen as neurodiverse include people with autism, those with ***ADHD*** (Attention Deficit Hyperactivity Disorder), ***Dyslexia*** (trouble with reading) and ***Tourettes*** (involuntary verbal sounds and movements), to name a few.

It’s said that men are more likely to have autism than women, which isn’t entirely true. Women are more able to cover their autistic traits, otherwise known as ***masking***. I unintentionally mask, which means I instinctively mimic behaviour in an attempt to appear “normal.” I also have an autism related sleeping disorder, meaning it is very hard for me to get a good nights sleep.

Due to systematic racism and sexism, it is also a lot harder for women, and people of colour to get a diagnosis. Because of this, they are often only diagnosed in adulthood, if they are diagnosed at all.

You may have heard people use the phrases “High Functioning” and “Low Functioning” when it comes to describing autism. These phrases are now being seen as harmful. What you could use instead is “***high support needs***” and “***low support needs***”, but remember just because someone’s support needs are low, they still need support nonetheless.

What do you think of when you think of an autistic person? Do you think of Sheldon Cooper? Or do you think of Leonardo Di Caprio as Arnie Grape? There are people on the autistic spectrum who are maths geniuses who are overly logical, and socially inept, and there are people on the autism spectrum who seem as if they have the mental age of a 5 year old. Though these representations have some basis in truth, autism is a broad spectrum, and if you’ve met one autistic person, you cannot meet another autistic person and expect them to have the same strengths and difficulties.

Being autistic doesn't mean we don't have personalities. We're humans, not emotionless robots with expert abilities (cough Rain Man cough). You might have seen autism be represented by a missing jigsaw piece, and I can assure you nothing in my head is missing, waiting to be found.

Unfortunately, autism hasn't been represented well at all in media, and the few films or shows which have characters with autism, often solely centre around this as the main figure of their personality. "Isn't that a good thing though?" Yes. We need stories about autism and neurodiversity, but we also need stories where disability isn't the forefront, and where characters aren't defined purely by their medical conditions.

A few things to remember to help Autistic people include:

- Not all disabilities are visible, especially a developmental disability.
- Please don't speak for us unless we ask you to, or are unable to.
- Don't talk over us, as if we are not in the room.
- Please be patient.

- Speaking isn't the only form of communication. Just because someone might be non-verbal, it doesn't mean they don't have a voice.

- Sharing our content. As mentioned, we're not very well represented in media. If you see something we've created, share it! Retweet it! Put it on your story! Lift our voices!

- If you are in a position to, employ us! 77% of autistic people are unemployed in the UK. We want to work. We are able to work. Create an inclusive and accommodating work place.

- Please don't try to fix us and search for a cure. We don't need to be fixed. What we do need is support, and patience. There are many therapies available to help us, without trying to cure us.

- Remembering autism can be difficult to deal with, but it isn't a burden. We can't help that we process the world differently. Autistic people are being murdered by people who are supposed to care for them.

10.

WHAT DO YOU THINK OF?

CONSENT AND PTSD

BY JACK HART

Consent is at the heart of human life. We are constantly negotiating with the people around us, setting ***boundaries*** and communicating them. In this piece I want to help you to understand what consent is and how it affects us every day, to empower you to set your own boundaries, as well as respect other people's.

I will speak about things such as ***sexual assault*** and ***Post Traumatic Stress Disorder***, so feel free to read at your own pace, take breaks, or come back to the article another day if you feel overwhelmed at all. This, by the way, is called a ***Trigger Warning***, and it's a subtle way to help flag up potentially distressing content, for people who might need it and find it useful.

What is Consent?

The Oxford English Dictionary defines consent as "permission for something to happen or agreement to do something." You might wonder why me; a white guy, is writing about consent. I have a lot of ***privilege***, which allows me assert my boundaries more than many other people, particularly women and people of colour. My voice is often immediately heard and respected because of my race and gender, so I want to give context. My journey with understanding my ***autonomy*** (the right to make our own decisions and have agency) has been complex. I was sexually assaulted by another student in a class at drama school, and as a result, have since developed Post Traumatic Stress Disorder (PTSD).

"PTSD is essentially a memory filing error caused by a traumatic event." In this filing error the traumatic memory does not get processed by the brain and can cause symptoms such as re-experiencing the event (flashbacks), ***dissociation*** (feeling 'out of body' or spaced out), nightmares and avoiding things which remind you of the distressing event.

1 in 2 people experience a traumatic event during their lifetime. Of those, around 20% can develop PTSD. For me the main symptom of my PTSD is constantly feeling unsafe. It impacts me every day in how I see myself, experience, and interact with the world.

What do you think of when you read the word consent? For many people the answer might be sex, or it could represent a lifesaving surgery, the terms and conditions on a new subscription, dancing with somebody in a club, a handshake or grab. We give or withhold consent all the time using our words, body language, voice and facial expressions. And we are constantly reading other people's boundaries through their choice of words and posture too.

Has anybody got that bit too close to you in the shops during the pandemic? You feel them reaching past you to get something off the shelf, rather than waiting for you to finish browsing the section, or asking you politely to move to the side. Some of us might have responded by quickly moving away and averting our eyes, others by flipping into a rage and shouting "Have you not seen the news? It's two metres!" and some of us might have frozen completely, staying still until the person has passed. We all respond differently when our brains perceive a threat. The differences are commonly referred to as fight, flight, freeze or flop.

In this example, the person has ignored us, broken the rules of social-distancing and prioritised their desires above our needs (***personal space***). They did not seek consent and therefore it might have made us angry, anxious, passive, unsafe or any range of feelings. Consent is about recognising that there is another human involved in what we want and giving them an opportunity to agree or decline.

Consent cannot be given unless you have been provided with the genuine option of saying no. This is why language can often be the clearest way to gain consent: "yes" is often clearer than a nod of the head. Equally, just because you don't hear a person say no, that does not mean they have consented. You should always clarify with the person if you are unsure whether they have consented to an act. What you are about to do could have huge implications for that person's life moving forward, whether it feels significant to you or not, and ultimately, depending on the act, you could end up with a criminal record and time in prison.

It's important to consider how much power we have in a room when we seek consent. By power I mean ***status***, which could be to do with your job, but also other influences you have over people. Is this person agreeing to this because they want to, or because they are scared of how you will respond to them saying no? This can apply to sex, but also touching a person's hair, standing close to somebody in your office, smelling them, fixing their collar, buying them coffee, or any number of acts. For example, in a student/ teacher relationship the teacher has more power than the student and the teacher must consider their intentions when asking something of the student. The student can of course behave abusively towards the teacher, but the teacher will always have the status of their job and role within the community behind them, which gives them power in the relationship.

I've heard some people say it's "a minefield," or that "you can't do anything these days," when the topic of consent is raised. To those people I encourage you to look inwards at your own life and ask "What is it about me that means I haven't had to worry about this?" The answer is usually something to do with: race, class, gender, sexuality, ability, or a combination of the above. And that's what privilege is. I personally don't experience discrimination because of my race, my gender or ability, but I have because of my class and sexuality.

Consent affects us all, every day.

Where are your boundaries? What are the things that make you feel uncomfortable or invalidated? Do the people around you know that? Would they be accepting if you shared these things with them?

What makes us comfortable and safe can be different from place to place and depending on who we're with, you don't need solid rules for life to set boundaries. But by starting to listen to your own body and figuring out what you need in order to feel comfortable and supported, then communicating that with the people around you, you can understand why it's important for other people, and in turn create a cycle of respect, which can increase productivity, improve wellbeing and reduce crime rates.

If this article has brought up any personal experiences for you, know that there are a range of services available for you to engage with. I've personally utilised the services of SurvivorsUK (a charity for male and non-binary survivors of sexual assault or abuse). They offer a free webchat and phone line as well as group therapy and one to one counselling services; and GALOP (a charity for LGBTQ+ victims of hate crime, sexual violence or domestic abuse). Other services include: Rape Crisis England and Wales and Safeline.

I want to end by recommending the incredible TV show I May Destroy You, which is available on BBC iPlayer. Written by and starring Michaela Coel, the show looks at sexual assault from lots of different angles including one male perspective and really interrogates what consent is and how deeply its impacts are engrained into our society. A heads up that some of the scenes can be really difficult to watch, so have a read of the trigger warnings in the episode descriptions if you are concerned.

I think we are in a new time when it comes to understanding the importance of consent – more people seem ready to start some of those difficult conversations, certainly more people have opened up about their experiences of abuse in recent years within the #MeToo movement. I hope we can continue those discussions and act to create a safer, more connected and more equal society.

11.

I NEVER ASKED TO BE AN ACTIVIST

AIDS AND HIV

BY HARRY REY

"Don't die of ignorance." The adverts said. At school, the word "gay" didn't exist. Queer, fag, poof, even "Harry Hoofter," were all banded about in the corridors and classrooms, but ***Section 28*** still meant teachers put their fingers in their ears when it came to dealing with homophobic bullying. In my time at high school, cut short because I couldn't stand the abuse anymore, the only time my identity was ever acknowledged was by my art teacher, Mrs Heampstead. She gave me one piece of advice: "Don't get AIDS. It's horrible. It's the worst way to die."

I remember it from TV, too. When Mark Fowler in EastEnders left the show to go off and die like a dog when his HIV treatment "stopped working." It would take years before I learned that's not a thing.

On TV, in films, even in books, HIV was treated as a dark and deadly plot twist which weaves its way into characters' lives like a modern-day morality play. "See? This is what happens when you don't play by the rules."

Life Expectancy

"If you ever have sex again, you can go to prison."

That's the first thing the nurse told me as a newly diagnosed 22-year-old. Some people don't remember their diagnosis date. I'm not so lucky: it was my birthday. The call had come the night before, minutes before I was due to head out the door celebrate my new-found freedoms. University was over and my future was wide open.

"It's serious," the nurse continued at the wonderfully named ***Centre for Infectious Diseases***. "You're a risk to any of your future partners."

Well she didn't need to worry about that. My partner wasn't returning my calls. The doctor was dead against starting treatment. "Nasty stuff, those pills," he bumbled through a stiff collar and a leather-patched tweed coat. "The life expectancy of people taking these pills is actually shorter than those who don't." And who can argue with the professor?

As weeks of torment dragged into months of misery, I didn't much care about the ghostings, the unanswered messages or, even worse, the pity dates. I just wanted someone to talk to. I used to spend whole nights trawling the chat rooms buried away in the darkest corners of the early 2000's internet searching for someone like me, just to talk to them. I didn't care about how they got it or if they'd found love. I just wanted to know, "how long do you have left?"

Life Changing

"What do you know about being undetectable?" A nice lady with the clip board asked me one day.

"I don't know what that is."

"You've never heard of it?"

I shook my head. She scratched down a few notes on her page.

"How long have you been HIV positive for?"

"Nearly three years now."

"And how many partners have you had in that time?"

I shook my head again.

"None?"

"None. I... I didn't think I was allowed. They said I'm, you know, a risk."

“All right.” She put down her clipboard, leaned across the coffee table and took hold of my hands. “You are not a risk. You are a person. And you’re allowed to love. Being ***undetectable*** is when an HIV positive person is on effective ***antiretroviral treatment***, the pills that stop HIV replicating in the body, and the virus can’t be detected in their body. We know that makes them ***uninfectious***, and there are studies going on right now that can prove that.”

Back at the surgery, the doctor laughed when I asked. “Why would someone put themselves at risk by having sex with you? If you infect your partner you can go to prison.”

It was then I realised the doctor’s job was to keep me alive, not to allow me to live.

“I want to start treatment.”

“It’s still too early. Your CD4 count is still above 500 copies. NHS guidelines only recommend treatment when your count falls below 350.”

“I’m not leaving this office without a bottle of Eviplera. It’s one pill a day, I think I can handle that.”

Just twenty-one pills later, I was undetectable. That’s all it took. The virus in my body was ***untransmittable***. Treatment prevents transmission. Suddenly I no longer felt like a walking bag of used needles. I wasn’t toxic anymore.

While on effective treatment, HIV has no discernible impact on your overall life expectancy. Being undetectable means there is zero risk of transmission to a sexual partner. Not almost zero. 0%. It's an absolute zero. Undetectable = Untransmittable. You can't pass it on.

I fell in between a generation gap. My doctors were raised on diets of treatment cocktails; pill burdens which used to harm as many patients as they helped. The doctors were so focussed on the absolute meaning of life expectancy, they forgot to say what to fill them with. The profit margins of HIV, like any disease, don't leave much room for anything other than cold, hard data. The doctors make decisions based on the information the drug companies give them; they weigh up side effects and cost efficiency. The place a value on the years of your life, both in terms of cost and quality. How many good years do you have left, and what's that going to cost the taxpayer? No wonder that back then, they didn't want to put a 22-year-old on treatment.

The Cost of Life

The world of HIV/Aids is very different today from when I was first diagnosed ten years ago. But some things about it haven't changed. Our chronic condition still sustains the livelihoods of tens of thousands of people, millions of shareholders, and billions in profits for drug companies.

Nothing illustrates the glaring health inequalities caused by the capitalisation of the Aids industry more than the case of Martin Shkreli, the "pharma bro," currently serving a seven-year prison sentence for securities fraud. In 2015, Martin Shkreli caused global outrage when his pharmaceuticals company Turing "bought" the rights to a lifesaving drug called Daraprim. The next time the NHS says they "can't afford" to provide a medicine, it's because the drug company has their shareholders to think about.

Daraprim (Pyrimethamine) has been available since 1953 although its patent long since expired. It used to cost $1 per pill, but in 2010 GlaxoSmithKline sold the marketing rights to CorePharma, which allowed Shkreli's company to swoop in, buy the rights and hike the price 5,000% to $750 per pill.

The world was rightly outraged, and headlines from the time said how despicable it was Shkreli had hiked the price of this vital "HIV" drug. But there's only a market for Daraprim because people are still developing AIDS, which in today's world doesn't need to happen. Treatment enables people living with HIV to stay virally suppressed and healthy for the rest of their lives, but in countries without adequate healthcare such as the US and parts of sub-Saharan Africa, treatment is not easily available. While in the UK, over 85% of all people living with HIV (whether they know it or not) are virally suppressed, in the US this figure is barely a third.

In the UK and countries with effective testing and treatment, most people with HIV have a lower overall death rate than people without HIV. And that's not just because treatment for HIV and AIDS-related illnesses is delivered free through the NHS. It's because other conditions which HIV positive people face, in particular Hepatitis C, are quickly dealt with. Unfortunately, this comes at great financial cost.

What Martin Shkreli did, although legal, was grossly unethical. But he's not the only one. He just got smacked about in the press for it. The greatest price gouging scandal of our time comes one of the world's biggest pharmaceutical companies - Gilead - and their Hepatitis C drug Sofosbuvir. It's a complete cure for the liver disease, and practically side effect free, unlike previous Hepatitis treatments. Gilead charges $1,000 per pill. A course of treatment can be up to 28 weeks, costing nearly $200,000 which makes it the most expensive drug ever sold. Gilead justifies it by saying they need to recoup their research and development costs, but that is stretching the truth.

A smaller company called Pharmasset had already developed this Hepatitis C cure and was testing it in various clinical trials. In 2011, Gilead swooped in and bought the company for $11bn. In just one year, Gilead made $14bn on sales of Sofosbuvir in the US alone. So yes, Gilead did recoup their costs, but like many pharmaceutical companies, their costs are not for labs and scientists, but stocks and shareholders, and the costs are passed on to thinly stretched national health services.

Owning life-saving treatments for deadly conditions is highly profitable. Why else is there a global race to be the first to find a COVID-19 cure? The story of HIV is a microcosm of the business of disease. First comes the plague, then comes the treatment, then comes the profits. The person - the individual with the condition, their hopes, their dreams, their fears, never enters into the equation.

Love Expectancy

I never asked to be an activist. I never asked to know about virus replication, RNA, and more drug names than a pop star's medicine cabinet. Just as I never asked to be infected with HIV. But here I am, still. Life will teach us what it wants.

But through it all, the most important lessons I've learned are not about public health or drug company research costs. They're about love. Love for your own life, for your own future, for your own love story, no matter what life throws at you.

Four years ago, I married my husband, who is HIV negative. The week after our wedding, I sat down to write. Not just my story, but the stories of other people like me. I haven't stopped since. Fifteen books (and counting) later, I've learned the stories we tell ourselves are how we understand our future. The story of AIDS used to be told in words of victimhood, of shame, of fear, of vastly shortened life expectancies. But that's not how

HIV positive people live, or love. We have our own stories, and it's about time we tell them.

12.

A FAMILY DIVIDED

IMMIGRATION

BY BSR

There is a childhood photograph that has been on my desk for some time. As I work away, I often glance over and it always makes me smile. As a lecturer of the photographic arts, there are a plethora of motivational images that I could favour but it is this one that has pride of place next to my computer. To the left of the frame, my enthusiastic mum beams to camera with open body language. To the right, my stoic dad looks on disgruntled with crossed arms. I am in the middle. As someone who identifies as "***Mixed Asian***," with an Indian, Thai and Chinese background, the composition of this image mirrors the mindset of the British immigrant community - we are open to integration while maintaining a degree of cautious segregation.

Now, many years later, my first-hand engagement with multicultural students from Europe, Asia and further afield, is fascinating. I find that a classroom acts as a microcosm for societal values. The perspectives, views and attitudes of my parents are still apparent in my immigrant students; however, several generations later these views do seem to have begun to be eroded.

Full Circle

"What you must understand, is that in my country, photography is just a job. There is no love or passion for it," one student explains to me in an Eastern European accent when we discuss her motivation to make work. She looks at me with unshaken intent. The stereotype of valuing pragmatism over creativity is commonplace within the ***first wave*** of immigrant communities. My Indian relatives presented me with the career choices of doctor, lawyer or engineer at school. I presume that this trend is based upon survival instinct – obtain a path that offers social prestige, guaranteed income and distinguishes you from the ***indigenous*** population. Any interest that I expressed in the arts was swiftly shunted. Now, as an educator myself, I am the first to offer support to my students who may be experiencing similar situations.

Even after making the decision to pursue a role within the creative industries, I still found myself superimposing Asian values over my actions. A tally of academic qualifications was my goal even though they do not steer success as a practitioner. My Eastern European student reminded me to be wary of this. She, like many, have the perception that a college certificate guarantees the life of their choice. In a bid to challenge them, I often arrange placements and career talks with working professionals. This is often for my benefit as well as theirs.

New Associations

My generation may have been the first to blend cultural references. When asked at school, "Where are you from?" I had no issue explaining that my heritage was a mixture of several countries, with Western media acting as a constant undercurrent that conflicted with an Asian identity. I relied upon phone calls to stay in touch with friends and relatives at home, whereas my students today have the benefit of the internet to spur their communications. Social media in particular represents a platform to coalesce artistic movements. Each swipe casts a vote for the fate of their photography with collaborators spread across the globe. Today a student is free to express a preference with any culture's tastes yet they always retain a fiery affinity with their country of origin.

As an educator, I am conscious to make students aware of British academic standards while tentatively displaying sensitivity for their individualisms. A dear mentor once told me a simple mantra, "Teach from what you know." It is something that has sat with me. As I construct lectures on my computer with the gaze of my parents from that photograph looking on, it is a conscious choice to be respectful of the upbringing that they gave me. I feel proud to contribute to the lives of my students. As immigrants, they are far removed from the tropes portrayed by the press. Each is hard working, entrepreneurial and brimming with creativity. It is highly rewarding to be a part of an educational system that empowers, supports and encourages a melting pot of immigrants, identities and nationalities, each of which inform and enrich other immigrants.

13.
CAPITALISM AND CLASS

A BRIEF OVERVIEW

We hear about capitalism all the time, but rarely do we stop and consider what it means, why it affects us, and how it links to inequality in the wider world. Capitalism is a huge subject and this is just the very simplest of overviews, but for a further exploration into some of the ideas considered here, we really recommend Jason Hickel's excellent book, *The Divide: A Brief Guide to Global Inequality and its Solutions*.

At its most basic, capitalism is a system whereby a country's trade and industry are controlled by private owners, rather than the government, for profit. People like to think of capitalism as survival of the fittest: those with the best ideas and products will make the most money and survive the longest. This, therefore, should encourage everyone to want to work hard, in order to achieve more. This is the basic premise on which our society works. As we earn more, we pay more tax and we also spend more.

The problem with capitalism is that, in reality, we can't all compete equally because we're not on an equal playing field. For a whole host of reasons, some people have access to resources which makes competing easier.

In an attempt to remove the negative consequences of capitalism, alternative ways of living have been suggested. The most well known of these ideas are communism and socialism. Although these terms are often confused and merged together, there are some essential differences. Both theories aim to limit worker exploitation: if your boss will make more money by you being productive, you're going to have to work harder while they get richer.

Karl Marx was an economist and philosopher who co-wrote the Communist Manifesto. Marx's central argument was that those who owned the means of production were exploiting the workers who helped generate their profit. As a result, this creates an imbalance: giving the owners power over the workers. Marx's solution was for workers themselves to collectively own the means of production, hence reducing the inequality gap.

In a socialist society, a democratic state controls the means of production. Rather than companies competing against one another, as in a capitalist society, socialism has workers contribute as much as they can, so that everyone can share in the benefits equally. However, this theory has been exploited by dictators such as Stalin and Lenin, and to this date there has never been a communist country.

Capitalism and class are inherently linked. In the 15th century, a typical peasant farmer was responsible for his own fare: perhaps he had some land and some animals; enough access to basic food and water through which to survive. Any money the peasant made, from selling wool, for example, was his to keep.

Wealthy nobles at the time began to get restless. England had a head start on the rest of the world due to the staggering wealth it had accumulated across the world as a direct impact of colonialism. The British Empire had invaded and taken over huge swathes of the world, stealing precious silver, gold and natural resources, which had helped to make it one of the richest nations on earth. Capitalism would claim that this was survival of the fittest, and that England must be naturally superior. However, we must not forget the enormous impact of slavery, which, apart from anything else, amounted to a colossal quantity of free human labour. England profited, not because it was somehow better than other countries, but because it specifically exploited those nations to make itself rich. It is an inequality that persists to this day.

Working for a wage seems normal to us now, but it was unheard of in the 15th century. Eager to earn more profits, the nobles of England came up with a cunning plan. They removed the centuries old rights to habitation and privatised huge swathes of the English countryside. This "enclosure" movement, saw vast portions of land fenced off for private use, displacing the peasants who had lived there for hundreds of years. Tens of millions of acres of land were acquired for private use, with the vast majority of the population being displaced. Displaced is a nice sounding word, which masks the horror and violence that accompanied this process, where villages and homes were burnt, and thousands were violently removed from their own land.

Wool and agriculture created huge opportunities for nobles looking to get rich. In their new private land, they created competitive markets for farmers, where leases were given to the farmers able to produce the most. Those who weren't able to compete were kicked off their land and left to fend for themselves. This process was known as "improvement," and peasants had to invent ways to extract more and more value from their land.

By the 19th century, almost no public land remained and a huge humanitarian crisis had been created by this drive for wealth. England had become a capitalist society, and while the rich grew richer, vast quantities of people had no where to live and no hope for better. This is the setting for Charles Dickens' *Oliver Twist*, and it was as bleak as he imagined.

As the rich grew richer and market competition increased, labour became cheaper due to the sheer competition for work. Alongside the profits from slavery and colonialism, Britain became an unequal society. A new dawn had arrived in world economics, as England's elite no longer needed to use force to create more profits, the sheer drastic conditions of the market they had created resulted in cheap labour and high productivity. Ironically, as the power of the market spread, the workers had little choice but to become consumers, as they increasingly had to buy the basic necessities with which to survive.

The working-class had been created. Seeing how well enclosure had worked in Britain, the elite soon turned their attention to Ireland where they tried a similar tactic there. By the time enclosure had removed so much of Ireland's land into private ownership, peasants resorted to planting potatoes as their primary means for survival. In 1845 The Great Famine killed 1 million people, more than 10% of the population, when the potato supplies were unable to grow. This was a completely unavoidable catastrophe caused exclusively by rich land-owners driving their workers for profit.

Inequality through class and land divisions exist to this day, with much evidence pointing to the fact that the gap is continuing to increase. In July 2020, Jeff Bezos, Amazon founder and world's richest man, added $10b to his fortune in just one day. In England, the cast-off of private land ownership means that 97% of land is privately owned, restricting our access from its health and wellbeing benefits. Western governments send millions in aid to so-called third-world countries, and simultaneously protect their interests to prevent the world-economy from ever tipping the balance of power away from Western favour. Perhaps only environmental catastrophe can change humanity's unequal fortunes, but at what cost?

14.
VEGANISM

A BRIEF OVERVIEW

Veganism is, "a lifestyle that avoids all animal foods such as meat, dairy, eggs and honey," as well as "animal derived products like leather; and as far as possible, products tested on animals."

There are several reasons why an individual may choose to become vegan, primarily related to personal health, climate concerns and animal welfare. There were more than 600,000 vegans in Britain as of 2018: a figure that has doubled twice within the past four years, as more and more people consider this lifestyle for themselves and their loved ones.

It is sometimes claimed that humans need meat in order to survive. We do require protein as part of a balanced and healthy diet, but it is perfectly possible and safe to live as a vegan, with a vegan diet being validated by the British Dietetic Association.

According to the Vegan Society, around 60 billion land animals and more than a trillion marine animals are used and killed for human consumption every year. Veganism upholds that this is a totally unnecessary cruelty inflicted on our fellow species, when alternative plant-based diets are fully possible for us to thrive on.

Animals raised for consumption are often killed prematurely and placed in unnatural conditions in order to extract the best quality meat and milk. This is often distressing to the animals involved. Despite popular assumptions, animals such as cows are highly intelligent and emotional creatures, who suffer hugely as a result of human farming.

The labour intensive effort of raising cattle, and the methane they produce, has a devastating impact on the earth's climate. As our overall global population continues to grow and as we tend to live longer, this has led many to claim that we simply cannot afford to continue to feed ourselves in the way that we have done in the past: the current method is unsustainable.

Although vegetarianism is commended, vegans believe that the treatment and ethics of all animal farming are problematic to a view that our world should be shared between all species. Ultimately, any animal raised for human consumption is an animal unnecessarily killed or treated in some degree of captivity, which is not deemed ethical to a vegan lifestyle.

15.
THE CLIMATE EMERGENCY

A BRIEF OVERVIEW

- Since pre-industrial times, the atmospheric concentration of Carbon Dioxide in the earth's atmosphere has increased by 30%. This means more heat is trapped inside the earth's atmosphere, resulting in global warming.
- Extreme weather, as a result of global warming, has a devastating impact on human life, livelihoods and the natural world. In the 1990's, some 600,000 deaths took place, worldwide, in connection with extreme weather.
- Short-term fluctuations in weather can also have a dramatic impact on human life, causing hypothermia and hyperthermia, as well as a range of respiratory diseases. It is thought that high temperatures across Europe in the summer of 2003 contributed to 70,000 excess deaths that year.

- Increased temperature also results in more pollen, which is bad news for hay-fever sufferers. This can trigger asthma, which affects some 300 million people worldwide.

- More than half of the world's population live within 60km of the shoreline. Rising sea levels, another byproduct of increased global temperature, has the ability to cause widespread displacement to those people who live in these areas. This will result in huge swathes of migrants, as communities are displaced, and apart from flooding, increased sea levels also brings a risk of higher disease transmission.

- With less predictable rainfall comes increased pressures on fresh water supplies. Currently 2.2 million people die each year of diarrhoea, which is expected to increase.

- The worst impacts of climate change could be irreversible by 2030. Bill McKibben, co-founder of 350.org, said, "we've wasted the three decades since we were first warned by scientists that the climate was changing in perilous ways."

- The 20 warmest years on record have all occurred within the last 22 years.

- It's not just humans who will be affected - over 1 million species are at risk of extinction as a result of climate change. As their homes are destroyed, they will not be able to adapt quick enough to a world changing before their very eyes.

- We are losing the equivalent of 30 football pitches a minute of our tropical rainforests. Most of this is done to provide further space for cattle farms and for the production of palm olive oil, which appears in a staggeringly large number of household products.

We are seeing increasing evidence of the climate emergency across the world. As a species, we are moving towards the most crucial stage in our battle to reverse climate change, and for this we need decisive action from leaders and governments. Unfortunately, this does not seem to be happening, and several world leaders and prominent figures continue to repeat the idea that climate change is a myth, or that it is a natural phenomenon not related to human activities. But the research and evidence proves this to be incorrect. Although climate change can seem like a difficult subject to grasp, and an even harder topic to have any personal impact with, there are several ways we can make individual changes to help. Being mindful of our diet is one of the simplest and most significant changes we can make to the environment, but if we continue to show our leaders that this issue is important to us, they will have to listen. We need to take action before it is too late.

16.
FUNDING YOUR EDUCATION

A BRIEF OVERVIEW

We often come across many myths and misinformation when it comes to financing university study and considering whether you can afford to go. University isn't the path for everyone, but you shouldn't close the door until you've looked through it, especially when it can be a lot more affordable than you may think.

Tuition fees, the amount you pay to study a course, have gone up a lot in recent years, with the average course now costing around £9,250 per year. That's a total of approx £27,750 over a typical three year course. This tends to make people think that university isn't for them, or that it could never be worth so much money. Let's break it down.

You can apply for a student loan which pays your tuition fee for you. Additionally, if you think you need some help with living costs, you can apply for a maintenance grant. If you're planning to move away from home, or if you're in London, you are entitled to a bit more. Your maintenance grant is means tested, meaning that it's based on your household income. This means that the support goes to those who need it most.

Although this means you leave university with an eye watering amount of debt, there are a few things to be aware of, which make a Student Loan a bit different from a typical lone from a bank.

- You only repay your loan when you're earning over a certain amount. Currently, this amount is £26,575, for students starting a course today. If you're earning less than that, or if you're unemployed, you won't pay a thing.
- Your student loan is written off thirty years after you start repaying it. If you become permanently disabled or die, your loan isn't passed on to someone else.
- You're entitled to more than three years of Student Finance. This means, in essence, that if you go to university and drop out, and then start a new course, you will be covered. You'll have another year of tuition fees to pay back, but it doesn't mean it's game over.
- You pay 3% interest on your student loan.

You need to be able to provide evidence of your household income and it can take a while to get your application sorted, but there is plenty of resources available. University prices have caught the news a lot in recent years, and while it is expensive, in reality, your debt doesn't affect you hugely. Think of university as an investment in yourself: if going to university will help you to earn a higher wage, paying back a few pounds a month will be worth it. Your loan is taken out of your pay packet automatically by your employer, just like your National Insurance or Pension contributions, so you don't have to do anything, and it's easier, as you barely notice it's gone.

Still not convinced?

There are many viable alternatives to university today and it's not the right route for everyone. However, if you're weighing up the options, here are a few things to consider to see whether the experience may be worth it for you.

- Teaching staff – who will be teaching you? Good universities are happy to advertise this: good staff will help you immensely, especially if they have relevant, recent work experience.

- Facilities – what equipment and facilities will you have access to as part of your course?

- Where do graduates end up? Don't be afraid to search and ask this during open days.

- Your world will literally grow – you will be in the amazing position of meeting people with the same career ambitions as you, probably from all over the world. This is great socially, but will also have a big impact on your connections and employment network in the future.

About The Editor

Karl Falconer is the General Manager of The PurpleDoor, a community theatre and performance space based in Liverpool, England. The PurpleDoor is the UK's first truly free theatre, which exists to showcase an alternative model for artistic innovation, creation and production. The work of the PurpleDoor is to champion working-class talent and regional voices, and to address the huge imbalance which currently exists in the UK creative industries. You can find out more about the work being done by the company at www.thedoorisopen.co.uk.

FURTHER RESOURCES

This is a ***reference*** section - it includes lots of examples of further reading, if you want to learn more about a subject. Our authors have all recommended resources which they think you might like - some are websites and articles, some are films and documentaries, so there's a wide range. Where possible, our authors have selected resources that are free to access. The BBC iPlayer and Chanel 4's catchup service, 4OD, are great places to find documentaries about a range of subjects, which can be a helpful start for your journey.

Each of these references lists the title of the piece, the author and a link. This makes it easy for you to find them. Most of the time, if you Google the title, you should find it. If you're in a library, head over to the non-fiction section.

FAKE NEWS

Unelected: The Insidious Influence of Rupert Murdoch at the Heart of Government, *Hacked Off* (https://hackinginquiry.org/unelected-insidious-influence-murdoch/).

The Quick Guide to Spotting Fake News, *Freedom Forum Institute* (https://www.freedomforuminstitute.org/first-amendment-center/primers/fake-news-primer/).

How to Fact Check Like a Pro, *University of West Florida* (https://libguides.uwf.edu/c.php?g=609513&p=4274530).

How to Identify Fake News, *Stop Hate UK* (https://www.stophateuk.org/how-to-identify-fake-news/).

Outfoxed, *Youtube* (https://www.youtube.com/watch?v= fTtkkAcTdg).

The BBC Should Admit its Mistake and Move On, *Guardian* (https://www.theguardian.com/media/commentisfree/2019/jan/27/question-time-bbc-diane-abbott).

The Rise of the Murdoch Dynasty, *BBC iPlayer* (https://www.bbc.co.uk/iplayer/episode/m000kxvz/the-rise-of-the-murdoch-dynasty-series-1-1-kingmaker).

How Rupert Murdoch's Empire of Influence Remade the World, *New York Times* (https://www.nytimes.com/interactive/2019/04/03/magazine/rupert-murdoch-fox-news-trump.html).

Dial M for Murdoch, by Tom Watson and Martin Hickman (Allen Lane, 2012).

Scandalous! The Tabloid that Changed America, *BBC iPlayer* (https://www.bbc.co.uk/iplayer/episode/m000kbnw/storyville-scandalous-the-tabloid-that-changed-america).

"There is No News Today": What a Change from 1930's to Today, *BBC News* (https://www.bbc.co.uk/news/entertainment-arts-39633603).

BBC Reality Check, *BBC Twitter*.

BLACK BRITISH HISTORY

Natives: Race and Class in the Ruins of Empire, by Akala (Two Roads, 2019).

Black and British: An Untold History, *BBC iPlayer* (https://www.bbc.co.uk/iplayer/episode/b082w9p9/black-and-british-a-forgotten-history-1-first-encounters).

Britain's Forgotten Slave Owners, *BBC iPlayer* (https://www.bbc.co.uk/iplayer/episode/b062nqpd/britains-forgotten-slave-owners-1-profit-and-loss).

The Divide: A Brief Guide to Global Inequality and Its Solutions, by Jason Hickel (Penguin, 2017).

Why I'm No Longer Talking to White People About Race, by Reni Eddo-Lodge (Bloomsbury, 2017).

13th, *Netflix* (https://www.netflix.com/gb/title/80091741).

A Little History of the United States, by James West Davidson (Yale University Press, 2015).

SEXUALITY

Stonewall (https://www.stonewall.org.uk/).

Best Practice Toolkits and Resources, *Stonewall* (https://www.stonewall.org.uk/best-practice-toolkits-and-resources-0).

How To Be LGBT Friendly, *Warwick University* (https://warwick.ac.uk/services/equalops/a-z/how to be lgbt friendly.pdf).

LGBT History, *Instagram* (https://www.instagram.com/p/CCTqP4nJ3A7/).

This Book Is Gay, by Juno Dawson (Hot Key Books, 2014).

50 Shades of Gay, *TedTalk* (https://www.ted.com/talks/io tillett wright fifty shades of gay).

A Guide for People Who Question Their Sexual Identity, *Your Sexual Orientation* (https://yoursexualorientation.info/).

LGBT Helpline, *Switchboard* (https://switchboard.lgbt/).

Am I Gay, Lesbian or Bisexual? *NHS* (https://www.nhs.uk/live-well/sexual-health/am-i-gay-lesbian-or-bisexual/).

MENTAL HEALTH

Reasons to Stay Alive, by Matt Haig (Cannongate Books 2016).

The Mountain, by Laura Ding-Edwards (That Guy's House, 2019).

*My Sh*t Therapist*, by Michelle Thomas (King's Road Publishing, 2019).

Depressive Illness: the Curse of the Strong, by Dr Tim Cantopher (SPCK, 2018).

The Power of Now, by Eckhart Tolle (New World Library, 2010).

Lost Connections, by Johann Hari (Bloomsbury, 2018).

A Tale of Mental Illness from the Inside, *TedTalk* (https://www.ted.com/talks/elyn_saks_a_tale_of_mental_illness_from_the_inside?language=en).

Hub of Hope, *Chasing the Stigma* (https://hubofhope.co.uk/).

HUMAN RIGHTS

What are the Universal Human Rights? *TedTalk* (https://www.youtube.com/watch?v=nDgIVseTkuE).

Human Rights in Two Minutes, *Amnesty Switzerland* (https://www.youtube.com/watch?v=ew993Wdc0zo).

What are Human Rights? *Amnesty International UK* (https://www.amnesty.org.uk/what-are-human-rights?utm_source=google&utm_medium=grant&utm_campaign=AWA_GEN_human-rights&utm_content=human%20right).

Amnesty Academy, *Amnesty International UK* (https://academy.amnesty.org/learn).

Creative Treaty (https://www.creativetreaty.org/).

The Human Rights Act, *Liberty* (*https://www.libertyhumanrights.org.uk/your-rights/the-human-rights-act/*).

Our Human Rights Act Explained in 2 Minutes, *The British Institute of Human Rights* (*https://www.youtube.com/watch?v=BOc-fpC1bak*).

What is the European Convention on Human Rights? *Amnesty International UK* (https://www.amnesty.org.uk/what-is-the-european-convention-on-human-rights).

We Are All Born Free, by Amnesty International (2011).

A is for Activist, by Innosanto Nagara (Seven Stories Press, 2016).

My Name is Not Refugee, by Kate Milner (Barrington Stoke Ltd, 2017).

The Journey, by Francesca Sanna (Flying Eye Books, 2016).

Azzi Inbetween, by Sarah Garland (Lincoln Children's Books, 2016).

Julian is a Mermaid, by Jessica Love (Walker Books, 2019).

Where the River Runs Gold, by Sita Brahmachari (Hachette Books Group, 2019).

Poems from a Green and Blue Planet, edited by Sabrina Mahfouz (Redcliffe, 2014).

Guantanamo Kid, by Sonia Laso (Harry N. Abrams, 2019).

Sensible Footwear: A Girl's Guide, by Kate Charlesworth (Myriad Editions, 2019).

Anti-hate Anthology, by Spoken Word London (2019).

How to Be an Antiracist, by Ibram X. Kendi (Random House, 2019).

The Lightless Sky, by Gulwarli Passarlay (Harper One, 2016).

TRANS IDENTITIES

How to Talk (And Listen) to Transgender People, *TedTalk* (https://www.ted.com/talks/jackson_bird_how_to_talk_and_listen_to_transgender_people#t-371089).

The Truth About Trans, *Stonewall* (*https://www.stonewall.org.uk/truth-about-trans#trans-people-britain*).

The Gender Spectrum: A Scientist Explains Why Gender Isn't Binary, *Cade Hildreth* (https://cadehildreth.com/gender-spectrum/).

Sex Isn't Binary, and We Should Stop Acting Like It Is, *Massive Science* (https://massivesci.com/articles/sex-gender-intersex-transgender-identity-discrimination-title-ix/).

Why Gender Neutral Pronouns Are Important, *Vogue* (https://www.vogue.com.au/culture/features/why-gender-neutral-pronouns-are-important/).

What Does It Mean to Be Non-Binary or Have Non-Binary Gender? *Very Well Mind* (https://www.verywellmind.com/what-does-it-mean-to-be-non-binary-or-have-non-binary-gender-4172702).

What It Means to Identify as Non-Binary, *Huffington Post* (https://www.huffingtonpost.co.uk/entry/non-binary_uk_5c04f8dae4b0606a15b6e448?utm_hp_ref=uk-being-non-binary).

A Short History of Trans People's Long Fight for Equality, *TedTalk* (https://www.ted.com/talks/samy_nour_younes_a_short_history_of_trans_people_s_long_fight_for_equality#t-361851).

Non-Binary People Aren't a New Phenomenon, *Huffington Post* (https://www.huffingtonpost.co.uk/entry/non-binary-travis-alabanza_uk_5c06aa1de4b0cd916fb0947d).

Here's What Older Trans and Non-Binary People Want You to Know, *Buzzfeed* (https://www.buzzfeednews.com/article/skarlan/heres-what-older-trans-and-nonbinary-people-want-you-to-know).

7 Famous Transgender People From History, *Spectrum Outfitters* (https://spectrumoutfitters.co.uk/blogs/spectrum-spotlight/7-famous-trans-people).

Transphobia Is a White Supremacist Legacy of Colonialism, *Medium* (https://medium.com/@Michael_Paramo/transphobia-is-a-white-supremacist-legacy-of-colonialism-e50f57240650).

Fuck Your Gender Norms: How Western Colonisation Brought Unwanted Binaries to Igbo Culture, *Gal-Dem* (https://gal-dem.com/colonialism-nigeria-gender-norms-lgbtq-igbo/).

Pay Us Some Mind: On the 'Tragic' Humanity of Black Trans Women, *Autostraddle* (https://www.autostraddle.com/pay-us-some-mind-on-the-tragic-humanity-of-black-trans-women-278402/).

Why Black Trans Women Are Essential to Both Pride and Black Lives Matter, *Yahoo Life* (https://www.youtube.com/watch?v=1SYWAPLJzkQ).

Into Black Trans Liberation, *NBC News* (https://www.nbcnews.com/podcast/into-america/transcript-black-trans-liberation-n1232931).

Make No Mistake - the Government Is Mandating State-Sponsored Violence Against Trans People, *Independent* (https://www.independent.co.uk/voices/transgender-gender-recognition-act-transphobia-liz-truss-boris-johnson-a9565416.html).

Inside the Great British TERF War, *Vice* (https://www.vice.com/en uk/article/889qe5/trans-rights-uk-debate-terfs).

Why We Take Issue With the Guardian's Stance on Trans Rights in the UK, *Guardian* (https://www.theguardian.com/commentisfree/2018/nov/02/guardian-editorial-response-transgender-rights-uk).

The Motherland of 'Gender Criticism', *Slate* (https://slate.com/human-interest/2019/12/rowling-transphobia-tweet-radical-feminism-discourse.html).

Tips for Allies of Transgender People, *Glaad* (https://www.glaad.org/transgender/allies).

Supporting Your Child With Gender Identity Issues, *Young Minds* (https://youngminds.org.uk/find-help/for-parents/parents-guide-to-support-a-z/parents-guide-to-support-gender-identity-issues/).

I Am the Parent of a Non-Binary Child, *Detroit Free Press* (https://eu.freep.com/story/opinion/contributors/2018/05/31/non-binary-gender-meaning/579154002/).

Dictionary of LGBTQ+ Terms, *Transvivor* (https://transvivor.com/dictionary).

POLITICS

They Work For You (https://www.theyworkforyou.com).

gov.uk (https://www.gov.uk/).

Ted Talks (https://www.ted.com/talks).

Panorama (https://www.bbc.co.uk/programmes/b006t14n).

The Open University (https://www.open.edu/openlearn/free-courses/full-catalogue).

The Week (https://www.theweek.co.uk/).

DISABILITY

Disability Rights UK (https://www.disabilityrightsuk.org/).

How to be an Ally of the Disabled Community, *Paraquad* (https://www.paraquad.org/blog/how-to-be-an-ally-of-the-disability-community/).

10 Ways to be a Good Ally to Disabled People, *She Might Be* (https://shemightbe.co.uk/10-ways-good-ally-disabled-people/).

Myths and Facts About People with Disabilities, *Easterseals* (https://www.easterseals.com/explore-resources/facts-about-disability/myths-facts.html).

Taxi Driver Training Pack, *DDSG* (http://www.ddsg.org.uk/taxi/language.html).

Disability Arts Online (https://disabilityarts.online/).

Graeae Theatre Company (https://graeae.org/our-work/).

Scope (https://www.scope.org.uk/).

British Sign Language (https://www.british-sign.co.uk/).

AUTISM

Float, *Pixar* (https://www.disneyplus.com/en-gb/movies/float/7dIYGyfvHWEJ).

Loop, *Pixar* (https://www.disneyplus.com/en-gb/movies/loop/5NfKNumn6L0l).

The A Word, *BBC iPlayer* (https://www.bbc.co.uk/iplayer/episodes/b09flzps/the-a-word).

There She Goes, *BBC iPlayer* (https://www.bbc.co.uk/programmes/b0bp2zq4).

Life Animated, *Netflix* (https://www.netflix.com/title/80097263).

Are You Autistic?, *Channel 4* (https://www.channel4.com/programmes/are-you-autistic/on-demand/65795-001).

Autie, *Kafabe* (https://www.youtube.com/watch?v=SRibeoE8HDA).

Autism in Pink, *The National Autistic Society* (https://www.youtube.com/watch?v=E-FvExDAqh8).

Things Not To Say To An Autistic Person, *BBC Three* (https://www.youtube.com/watch?v=d69tTXOvRq4).

Can you make it to the end?, *The National Autistic Society* (https://www.youtube.com/watch?v=aPknwW8mPAM).

Autistic and Unapologetic (https://autisticandunapologetic.com).

National Autistic Society (https://www.autism.org.uk).

CONSENT AND PTSD

Survivors UK (https://www.survivorsuk.org/).

GALOP (http://www.galop.org.uk/).

Rape Crisis England and Wales (https://rapecrisis.org.uk/).

Safeline (https://www.safeline.org.uk/).

Is This Sexual Harassment?, *BBC iPlayer* (https://www.bbc.co.uk/iplayer/episodes/p06x0jv5/is-this-sexual-harassment).

I May Destroy You, *BBC iPlayer* (https://www.bbc.co.uk/iplayer/episodes/m000jyxy/i-may-destroy-you).

Tea Consent, *Blue Seat Studios* (https://www.youtube.com/watch?v=oQbei5JGiT8).

The Power of Vulnerability, *TEDTalk* (https://www.youtube.com/watch?v=iCvmsMzlF7o&t=2s).

What is PTSD, Exactly? *Life Noggin* (https://www.youtube.com/watch?v=qOkJeAbddDw).

Daring Greatly, by Brené Brown (Penguin, 2012).

Trauma Is Really Strange, by Steven Haines (Jessica Kingsley Publishers, 2015).

The Body Keeps The Score, by Bessel Van Der Kolk (Penguin, 2015).

HIV AND AIDS

Terrence Higgins Trust (https://www.tht.org.uk/).

U=U Undetectable, *i-Base* (http://i-base.info/u-equals-u/).

What is PrEP?, *I Want PrEP Now* (https://www.iwantprepnow.co.uk/).

U=U, *George House Trust* (https://ght.org.uk/Undetectable).

Myths About HIV and Aids, *Avert* (https://www.avert.org/hiv-transmission-prevention/myths).

HIV and AIDS: Transmission Myths and Facts, *Medical News Today* (https://www.medicalnewstoday.com/articles/323832).

IMMIGRATION

Stateless, *Netflix* (https://www.netflix.com/gb/title/81206211).

Once Upon a Time in Iraq, *BBC iPlayer* (https://www.bbc.co.uk/iplayer/episode/m000kxwq/once-upon-a-time-in-iraq-series-1-1-war).

Immigration, *Full Fact* (https://fullfact.org/immigration/).

8 Facts About Migration You Won't Hear in the Media, *Global Citizen* (https://www.globalcitizen.org/en/content/facts-migration-immigration-impact-uk-tabloids/?gclid=Cj0KCQ_jwvIT5BRCqARIsAAwwD-Su7OHizSrIKUhtdK3jMK3w-51d0oIPd92FIIPzU7AvlA0kWoWS9kEaAk5bEALw_wcB).

Factfulness: 10 Reasons Why Things Are Better Than You Think, by Hans Rosling.

Britons Are Overwhelmingly Swayed by Myths About Immigration, *Independent* (https://www.independent.co.uk/voices/immigration-britain-channel-crossing-migrants-asylum-seekers-refugees-aid-a8713986.html).

Hostile Environment, by Maya Goodfellow (Verso Books, 2019).

CPSIA information can be obtained
at www.ICGtesting.com
Printed in the USA
LVHW090234090920
665411LV00002B/596